CHANCE ENCOUNTERS

Photographs from the Collection of
Norman Carr and Carolyn Kinder Carr

\

Cover: Leon Levinstein, *Rockefeller Center*, 1956

Károly Escher, *Napsugaras tavasz a korzón* (Sunlit spring day on the promenade) [variant], c. 1930

Corcoran Gallery of Art
Washington, D.C.

CHANCE ENCOUNTERS

Photographs from the Collection of
Norman Carr and Carolyn Kinder Carr

PAUL ROTH

FOREWORD
PAUL GREENHALGH

ESSAY
NORMAN CARR AND
CAROLYN KINDER CARR

Corcoran Gallery of Art
500 Seventeenth Street NW
Washington, DC 20006
www.corcoran.org

This book is produced in a limited edition.

This copy is number **327** of 500.

BOOK CREDITS
ACKNOWLEDGEMENTS

Published in conjunction with the exhibition *Chance Encounters: Photographs from the Collection of Norman Carr and Carolyn Kinder Carr*, Corcoran Gallery of Art, Washington, D.C., March 29–June 22, 2008. Organized by Paul Roth, curator of photography and media arts, Corcoran Gallery of Art. This exhibition is supported by the President's Exhibition Fund.

© 2008 by the Corcoran Gallery of Art.

Norman Carr and Carolyn Kinder Carr essay © 2008 by Norman Carr and Carolyn Kinder Carr.

Photographs sequenced by Paul Roth, John deWolf, and Amanda Maddox.

Edited by Amanda Maddox and Philip Brookman.

Copyedited by Sara Beth Walsh.

This book is printed by Anaconda Press in Forestville, Maryland.

The text in this book was set in Minion. Titles and headers were set in Gotham.

ISBN 0-88675-081-4

Norman Carr and Carolyn Kinder Carr would like to thank the following people:

First and most importantly, John Coplans (1920–2003), who started the process for us.

The dealers who helped educate us and focus our attention on specific artists and images, particularly Peter MacGill, Jeffrey Fraenkel, Howard Greenberg, and Gerd Sander.

Lou Stettner and Hendrik Berinson, who (along with John Coplans) helped us understand Weegee and his work.

Joe Mills, who mentored Norman's personal street photography and thus helped increase his understanding of how photographs are shot, selected, and printed.

The staff of the Corcoran Gallery of Art, in particular: curators Paul Roth and Philip Brookman, for encouraging the collection and offering advice in recent years on the acquisition of specific images; and Paul Greenhalgh, director and president, for his support of this exhibition and book.

Paul Roth would like to thank the following people at the Corcoran Gallery of Art: Paul Greenhalgh, Sam Sweet, Philip Brookman, Chris Leahy, Elizabeth Parr, Nancy Swallow, and Steve Taylor. He would also like to thank the Corcoran staff members who worked on the exhibition: Jennifer Adams, Ken Ashton, Reuben Breslar, Steve Brown, John deWolf, Ila Furman, Kristin Guiter, Maria Habib, Cory Hixson, Devon MacWilliam, Amanda Maddox, Mike McCullough and his team, Katy Murnane, Chris Nitti, Marc Roman, Andrea Romeo, Susan Ross, Darci Spasojevich, Charles Sthreshley, Susie Stockwell, Ellen Tozer, Sara Beth Walsh, Jason Zimmerman, and Marjory Zimmerman. Additional thanks to Alan Abrams and Mark Gulezian for their help with the production of this catalog.

Harry Callahan, *Chicago*, 1948

DIRECTOR'S FOREWORD
PAUL GREENHALGH
DIRECTOR AND PRESIDENT

This book accompanies an exhibition devoted to art from a single private collection. This is a rare enterprise indeed for us here at the Corcoran Gallery of Art, but one we are proud to undertake when the collection is as extraordinary as that featured in these pages.

Art collectors are as varied and independent as one can imagine. Norman Carr and Carolyn Kinder Carr have devoted themselves over a period of many years to building a collection of photographs with the scope of an historical survey. Picture by picture, idea by idea, and decade by decade, they have acquired great works of street photography with a view toward telling a story of the form. The parts were acquired, from early on, with anticipation of the whole. It is rare to find such focused, determined, and learned collectors.

When asked to explain the origins of their passion, serious art collectors often say that their compulsion to acquire art is not easily described in words. It is worth examining the whole of a collection to seek an image of those who assemble it. Norm Carr is tenacious and patient, salutary character traits befitting a former attorney. He is also a serious photographer, one who makes precisely the kind of imagery he collects. His wife Carolyn is methodical and critically-minded, a museum curator, administrator, and writer by trade and temperament. It goes without saying that Norm and Carolyn are both intensely interested in the ideas, history, and insights they discover through their photographs. One cannot build such a collection without serious dedication.

The Corcoran's photography exhibitions, and its collection, place it among the leaders in the museum world. The Corcoran has a proud record—now becoming an established tradition—in the world of photography. We have a substantial collection, we regularly stage large-scale temporary exhibitions, and we train photographers to degree level in our wonderful College. Our curators and faculty have depended throughout this history on the support of extraordinary collectors like the Carrs. This is true not just in the sense that we acquire work for our collection from such relationships, but also in that it helps us expand our own knowledge of the field. The best collectors contribute mightily to the shaping of the museum's collections and exhibitions, to scholarship and to the creation of photography. In short, they are key to the formation of the history of the art.

It is to the town, I think, to the town's prodigality

of incident and unsurpassable fluidity, that the

Photographer of the Future will turn most frequently.

The constant flux of her protean roadways,

the intricacies of her disordered buildings,

her passion for surprises—these are all

characteristics which commend her to the camera. [1]

—John Dixon Scott, 1906

Seeking an explanation

"Street photography" is a descriptive term for a type of documentary photography that incorporates elements of portraiture, reportage, and landscape. In simplest terms, it can be summed up as "candid pictures of everyday life in the street,"[2] but street photography is not easily described in any one way. At its heart, street photography is a hybrid, a form that has become more complex and irresolvable as it has evolved.

Street photography's curious development can usefully be analogized by reference to *film noir*, a subset of the crime movie genre that emerged in early 1940s Hollywood. In fact, many art historians have compared the two directly. Like *film noir*, street photography is a deliberately ambitious and ambiguous form of expression, designed to transcend description and storytelling to evoke the very nature of its subject. It is more realistic and yet more stylized than its antecedents, more subversive and ultimately more profound.

Street photography began in the late 19th century, evolved through the industrial age, and reached maturity between the two world wars; and it has developed over time in the service of social activism, journalism, documentation, illustration, and the making of art. This book is a selective survey of the form, drawn exclusively from a single private collection: that of Norman Carr and Carolyn Kinder Carr.

The Carrs have collected works from the early 20th century forward, but their choices throughout incline to an understanding of the genre's overall trajectory toward irresolution. Emphasizing scenes of human drift, the unpredictability of events, and chance encounters, the Carrs' collection is particularly sensitive to the mysterious. Whenever possible, they have acquired photographs that raise questions rather than provide answers. This essay explores their collection as a series of prompts—a set of provocations toward understanding the nature of street photography.

It is both self-evident and a bit of a mystery why a particular type of photography would emerge around the depiction of such a generic and everywhere-present location. Yes, the "street" (as a place both local and universal) is an apt and available subject for the camera, and has been throughout the world since the medium's

1   John Dixon Scott, "The Function of the Camera," in *Photography: Essays and Images*, ed. Beaumont Newhall (New York: The Museum of Modern Art, 1980), 202.

2   Colin Westerbeck and Joel Meyerowitz, *Bystander: A History of Street Photography* (Boston: Little, Brown and Company, 1994), 34.

Berenice Abbott, *Flatiron Building*, c. 1930-1933

beginnings in 1839. More importantly, though, the street is a symbolic locus, a shared reality, an arena for encounter, a place between places, a public gathering, an unfolding spectacle, an organizing principle, and a state of mind.

Concurrence: Lewis Hine and Weegee

In 1913, on the eve of the First World War, photographer and social reformer Lewis Hine, a pioneering activist for the poor, photographed children at work in factories, mills, canneries, mines, and on the streets of urban America on assignment for the National Child Labor Commission (N.C.L.C.). A long-time New Yorker, Hine found many of his subjects among lower-class neighborhoods and working districts on the Lower East Side.

That same year, immigrant teenager Arthur Fellig, the 14-year-old son of a pushcart vendor, had been in the country only four years when he began selling candy after school to help support his family. (A year later, he would drop out of school and leave home, striking out on his own to work—a common course for poor children.) The first customers for his candy were other children like himself, forced by their parents into labor in the factories of lower Manhattan. Fellig approached them at the end of their long shifts.

It is a peculiar fact that Fellig—who would later become "Weegee the Famous"—and his young customers were among the impoverished working children who made up Hine's principal subject group. Unfortunately, there is little possibility of knowing whether their paths ever crossed, and whether Fellig is included among the thousands of young people Hine photographed on the street. But it is interesting to imagine a young Weegee selling candy to the same children whose faces we see in Hine's emblematic images.

The city emerges as a subject

The architecture and activity of the modern city offered a ready-made subject for photographers at the turn of the 20th century. The city's multiplicity of subjects, the geometrics of its buildings, and the redefinition of public life in and along its streets combined to make a constantly evolving spectacle. The pace of economic expansion and the rise of industry brought more people and required more systemization and governance. The introduction of the automobile changed the sights and sounds of the streets; the upward thrust of new buildings placed transport and pedestrian passageways in relief. Towers of stone, cement, steel, and glass loomed over the increasing (and increasingly varied) populations below.

City streets, seen more and more as arenas for human interaction, had been rich sources of subject matter for Impressionist painters working in Paris in the late 1800s. By the 1920s, early Modernist painters and designers throughout Europe and in the United States drew primary inspiration from the city, from both its ferment of life and its rectilinear forms. Industrial-age glorification of the machine elevated the status of the camera, and artists began to see photography as a medium perfectly correlated to depict the modernizing forces at work in urban areas. "It would seem that only the camera is capable of reflecting contemporary life," Alexander Rodchenko observed in 1928.[3]

While the complex visual properties of cities held considerable attraction for photographers, many found a new subject in the public life of open areas. Parks, plazas, sidewalks, and city squares teemed with constantly shifting concatenations of people united in these spaces despite differences of class, ethnicity, language, and geographic origin. Men and women, young and old, wealthy and poor: in many cities people mixed as never before. Some photographers began to use their cameras to investigate both the differences and the commonalities evident among rising urban populations. In their work, the city's chaos echoed a struggle for life.

Urban discontents

As people moved from rural areas to towns and cities, pooling their resources and their labor in ever-greater concentrations around means of production, photographers used their cameras to document the discontents of the urban economy. The first-ever newspaper photograph, reproduced as a half-tone engraving, accompanied an article about urban poverty in New York's *Daily Graphic* on March 4, 1880. Ten years later, Danish-American social reformer Jacob Riis published his book *How the Other Half Lives*, supporting his text with photographs of tenement life in New York City. A pioneering work of sociology, it helped shape public awareness of conditions facing the poor.

Only 14 years separate Riis' book from Lewis Hine's first photographic project. In 1904, Hine, a young sociologist, began photographing new immigrants to New York, first at Ellis Island's port of entry and then in the same tenement neighborhoods Riis had

3 Alexander Rodchenko, "The Paths of Modern Photography," in *The Education of a Photographer*, eds. Charles Traub and Steven Heller (New York: Allworth Communications, Inc., 2006), 3.

depicted (see page 23). However, Hine's environmental portraits of immigrants and working children had aesthetic and philosophical resonance beyond their immediate utility as visual documents.

Hine's vision was rooted in the Ethical Culture movement, founded in the late 1800s to harness religious idealism and humanism to modern-age educational imperatives. Hine, who taught at New York's Ethical Cultural School, saw the camera as a tool of inquiry, a socially progressive means for revealing the burgeoning problematics of the modern state. At the same time, his vision was an ennobling one, and he set out to make portraits that would depict human perseverance in the face of struggle. While his images are characterized by a startling specificity of detail, they often bear a notably emblematic quality as well, standing simultaneously as icons of the suffering they depict and the empathetic viewpoint they represent.

Modernist aesthetics extend a social vision
In 1907, the same year Hine began his child labor project, he welcomed a promising new student to his photography classes at the Ethical Culture School: 17-year-old Paul Strand. That year, Hine took his students to meet photographer and art dealer Alfred Stieglitz at his Little Galleries of the Photo-Secession (291). While most details of the visit are lost to history, it seems likely that Stieglitz would have shown his groundbreaking city street scenes of the last 15 years, given their correlation with Hine's interests. Strand's own awestruck memory of the encounter makes it clear that one fateful field trip provided the twin wellsprings of his mature photographic vision, bringing the

humanist concerns of Ethical Culture progressivism into contact with aesthetic Modernism.

Strand immediately became a serious photographer, and some of his earliest subjects were found on the streets of New York. His influential city scenes from 1915 to 1917 combined social concern with a graphic interest in the city's activity. In photographs of street movement, particularly his famous 1915 image of workers walking on Wall Street, Strand portrayed a social flux that curator and photo historian Sarah Greenough described as "warring forces at times verging on chaos, of transience and impermanence opposed to the solidity of the physical structure of the city."[4] However, the graphic qualities of these photographs are not mere Modernist stylistics. Rather, Strand envisions a city's movement as its defining nature, a physical actualization of the tension between its citizens and its economic and social systems, as symbolized by the buildings looming overhead.

Tightly cropped portraits such as *Man, Five Points Square*, 1916 (see page 24) depict poor people with a kind of aggressive naturalism that is still jarring today. Strand took many of his street portraits in the rough neighborhood of Five Points, using a false lens to capture his subjects unawares. Strand's aesthetic viewpoint, like Hine's, is also ethical: these are iconic portrayals of marginalization. A person's isolation within the ebb and flow of the mainstream becomes a kind of freedom and, in Strand's eyes, a badge of honor.

Social classification
Though rarely identified as such, August Sander's monumental project *Menschen des 20. Jahrhunderts*

4   Sarah Greenough, *Paul Strand: An American Vision* (Washington, D.C. and New York: National Gallery of Art in association with Aperture Foundation, 1990), 35.

(*People of the 20th Century*) is also a key work in the development of street photography. In more than 600 portraits, Sander's ambitious taxonomy of German society portrays the modern face of a nation in the early years of a new century. In single photographs such as *Dachdeckermeister* (Master Roofer), 1930, and *Fellhändler* (Dealer in Skins), 1930 (see pages 25 and 27), Sander used his camera to observe individual details of clothing, physiognomy, professional attributes, and settings. Grouped within more than 45 categories in seven volumes, however, the sitters are portrayed generically, as fixed particulars within a collective.

Sander titled his photographs according to his sitters' professions, denoting their social identities rather than familial lineage. He often portrayed people in groups, showing carnival workers, street performers, intellectuals, political activists, families, schoolchildren, vagrants, and others alongside their peers. Interestingly, Sander frequently posed his subjects in public, using exterior settings such as roads, sidewalks, building walls, and city streets to place his subjects within a social realm (Sander's largest subject grouping, "Die Großstadt," or "The City," is devoted to urban life). Though sometimes only glimpsed, these common, repeated backgrounds connect metaphorically from one picture to the next: Sander's individuals are members of a public. They live with each other, constituents in a group portrait of modern life.

Concurrence: 1935–1936

The 1930s were fruitful years for street photographers. In the United States an economic depression caused widespread suffering, and in Europe a war began. The tumult of the era was especially evident in cities,

though the effects were everywhere, and everywhere visible to the lens. Advances in technology and publishing simplified the making and dissemination of documentary photography by this time, most notably the 1914 introduction of the Leica, a hand-held 35 mm roll-film camera; and the 1919 appearance of New York's *Illustrated Daily News*, the first daily newspaper to routinely reproduce photographic imagery.

From 1935 to 1936, an extraordinary period of ferment produced three organizations: a federal propaganda program, a socially-concerned photographer's collective, and a corporate media outlet. Each would dramatically influence the development of street photography.

In 1935, Roy Stryker, an American economist working in Franklin Delano Roosevelt's administration, began his famous federal photography initiative to document and promote economic recovery under the New Deal. His project was situated in the Information Division of the Farm Security Administration. Photographers working for Stryker's project depicted people living in poverty and chronicled the progress of federal economic initiatives in both urban and rural areas. During the Second World War, the project was moved to the Office of War Information; staff photographers chronicled life on the home front and American mobilization for war. The Carr Collection includes photographs made for the FSA/OWI by Walker Evans, Dorothea Lange, and Esther Bubley.

The next year, in 1936, the Photo League was founded by a group of photographers from the dissolving left-wing New York Film and Photo League. Among the photographers in the Carr Collection, Berenice Abbott, Margaret Bourke-White, Lewis Hine,

Leon Levinstein, Lisette Model, Paul Strand, Dan Weiner, and Weegee are all identified with the League, an educational group and artists' collective organized around its members' belief that documentary photography could provoke social change.

That same year, Henry Luce, publisher of *Time* and *Fortune*, introduced *Life*, beginning the era of mass-circulation picture magazines. The widely-read magazine elevated the importance of documentary and news photography and helped popularize the photographic essay, particularly during the Second World War and the middle-class economic renaissance of the 1950s. Among artists in the Carr Collection, Margaret Bourke-White and Robert Capa produced their most influential work on assignment for *Life*, and others like Henri Cartier-Bresson, Robert Frank, and Weegee made photographs that appeared in its pages.

Stryker's project continued through 1944; the Photo League dissolved in 1951 under government pressure during the McCarthy era; and *Life* appeared on newsstands until 1972. During their life spans these three entities produced very different imagery. The FSA/OWI photographers had been selected by Stryker for their ability to produce earnest, direct documentation of labor, poverty, and the capacity to overcome hardship. Their best-known work has a characteristic hard-bitten quality of observation. A socio-humanist ethos prevailed in the Photo League, one indebted to the traditions of Hine's Ethical Culture. League photographers, most of them New Yorkers and many of them Jewish, worked in the service of that ethos, making images that exposed the depredations of capitalism or heralded the common man. The editors of *Life* magazine published many different kinds of

photography, but they favored a style of pictorial reportage that was both specific and emblematic, illustrating particular stories and events while standing for commonly-understood heroic qualities.

As different as these enterprises were, much of the photography they produced was imbued with a politically progressive spirit. However, the improved production and dissemination of photographic images brought a greater degree of professionalism, and, by extension, predictability. Increasingly popular, documentary photography also became increasingly conventional. Some artists began to chafe against these conventions, and to define themselves against their colleagues, the magazines that published their work, and the expectations of their audiences.

Four photographers

Street photography came into its own in the 1930s and 1940s in the work of a few photographers whose vision transcended traditional documentary approaches. Their photography was not easily read as social activism or as journalism, though it contained elements of both. A binary complexity prevailed in their viewpoint; a sense that, in the words of curator and photo-historian Colin Westerbeck, "the world [in the picture] is both the public one of the street where the photograph was taken, and the private one of the subconscious where the composition was formed." [5] Their cameras were tools for description, but they were also instruments of revelation.

Henri Cartier-Bresson, photojournalist and artist, combined the leftist's embrace of the everyday with the surrealist's appetite for the extraordinary. Whether in Paris, his home city, or traveling the world in search

5   Colin Westerbeck and Joel Meyerowitz, *Bystander: A History of Street Photography* (Boston: Little, Brown and Company, 1994), 155.

of stories, he used his camera to compose remarkable scenes from the flow of life: "[Cartier-Bresson] is the unobtrusive witness who recognizes pictorial possibilities as they present themselves to his eye ... Objects seem to compose themselves as if by magic for him," wrote photo historian Beaumont Newhall in 1947. [6] The freedom and disorder of the city were first principles for Cartier-Bresson. Life seems to burst against the edges of his images, the elements held in perfect tension, inchoate and forever irresolvable. Looking at his photographs, one has the distinct sense of glimpsing a dream of reality, fraught with significance just beyond the reach of the conscious mind (see page 29).

Walker Evans saw the street as the arena of the ordinary, and he embraced what he saw in its minute particulars (see pages 30–32). With the factual vision of an anthropologist, Evans heralded what was unique in the common features of everyday life, once thought too minor or even too vulgar to portray in art: commercial signs, advertising posters, architectural details, power lines, living spaces, work clothing and uniforms, tools and utensils, and so on. He portrayed these details in layers so dense with information they suggest life's disorder. Evans' precise and respectful rendition of visual chaos implied a kind of favor, a valorization of the indigenous and the vernacular.

Weegee documented the streets of New York as a kind of visual detective and prosecutor, collecting evidence and filing indictments. A tabloid newspaper photographer by profession, he was a satirist by temperament, and his images reveal a burlesque of tragedy and absurdity playing out on the streets of New York (see pages 34–39). Though nominally

6   Beaumont Newhall, "Vision Plus the Camera: Henri Cartier-Bresson," in *Photography: Essays and Images*, ed. Beaumont Newhall (New York: The Museum of Modern Art, 1980), 284.

Weegee (Arthur Fellig), *Anthony Esposito, Accused "Cop Killer,"* January 16, 1941

a realist, Weegee's low origins, appetite for joy, and muckraking conscience inflect his photographs with a nakedly subjective and emotional core. His viewpoint is seemingly self-contradictory, both corrosive and sentimental, cynical yet full of faith. Having grown up in the same streets he photographed, Weegee seems all-knowing—not just in the sense that he always knows where the action was, but in that his vision is so capacious and confident, so sure of its conclusions. Weegee's work pities the poor and disdains the rich. Workingmen are noble; criminals get what they deserve. Fun is deliverance. In Weegee's universe, flashbulb bursts are like revelations, illuminating the instant when chance brings everyday events into alignment with larger truths.

Lisette Model, daughter of a wealthy Viennese landowner, took up photography as a commercial vehicle but rapidly developed an incendiary and misanthropic vision. "Promenade des Anglais," her excoriating 1934 series of portraits along the beach boardwalk of Nice, France, depicts an insolent upper crust, decomposing in cruelly-revealing sunlight. Arriving in the United States in 1938, Model shifted from European decadence to American vulgarity, making a brutal series of portraits of working and middle-class people on the streets of New York. Looming with misshapen bodies and contorted faces, her Expressionist satires echo the canvases of such German Expressionist painters as Otto Dix, George Grosz, and Ernst Ludwig Kirchner. Through Model's jaundiced lens, even wartime rallies are depicted with grim determinism: her subjects' patriotism shamed into submission by foreknowledge of death (see pages 42 and 43).

These four photographers were among the most important figures of documentary photography during the 1930s and 1940s, and yet they were artists first and foremost. None was entirely comfortable with the social purpose of their genre alone. Evans may have spoken for them all when in later years he said that he had "established the documentary style as art in photography." The camera's realism, in the hands of these photographers, was co-opted to very personal visions of the world.

(see pages 42 and 43).

Concurrence: 1955

In 1955, Edward Steichen, photographer turned curator of the Museum of Modern Art's photography department, mounted his landmark omnibus exhibition, *The Family of Man*. Viewed by more than nine million people during its lengthy international tour, the exhibition included 503 photographs by 273 photographers. It was intended as an epic expression of the humanist worldview that had played such a significant role in the rise of documentary photography. Not surprisingly, many photographers regarded Steichen's show as platitudinous and anachronistic. The show's aesthetic expression of political progressivism seemed inadequate, perhaps even less than truthful, in the aftermath of two world wars and the atomic bomb. Documentary photography was already moving in a different direction.

The same year MoMA exhibited *The Family of Man*, two different artists, working independently, embarked on the making of the two books that would come to define postwar street photography. One, William Klein, had not been included in Steichen's show; the other, Robert Frank, contributed a few pictures. Both had spent the postwar years nurturing a distrust of conventional documentary aesthetics—precisely those on view in Steichen's exhibition. Both saw the street as inherently expressive of uncomfortable truths, and both believed the difficulty of the subject demanded a new approach.

A native New Yorker, William Klein began photographing the city's boroughs only as a visitor, on a 1955 trip from his home in Paris, where he had lived since 1948. In a mere three months, Klein made the photographs for his incendiary 1956 book, *Life is Good and Good for You in New York: Trance Witness Revels*. Abrasive, raw, filled with motion, and hot with satire, Klein's grainy images were stylistically indebted to Weegee and Lisette Model, but their intellectual cynicism was something entirely new. Klein saw the city as inherently relentless, an inculcator of brutality where individuals crowd one another in increasingly combustible tension. The streets' bustle, commercialism, and amusement are viewed as enervating, suggesting an unbearable numbness and ennui (see page 52).

For all the visual dynamism Klein found in street life, his photographs suggest a depressingly mechanistic view of life. In this view of New York City, chaos—far from being an expression of freedom—becomes a blind struggle against larger social forces. The game is rigged. Klein's images were intended as a provocation, an assault on both subject and viewer. In fact, confrontation is a leitmotif of the book. In one scene, an adult, his face out-of-frame, points a toy gun at the head of a child; in another, a child points his toy gun at the camera, and at us. No documentary photographer had made such nihilistic pictures.

Just as Klein arrived in New York, photographer Robert Frank, a recent transplant to the city from Switzerland, embarked cross-country on a journey supported by a Guggenheim Fellowship. Hundreds of rolls of film made over two years yielded the 83 photographs of *The Americans* (1959), perhaps the single most important photography book of the postwar era. Frank's pictures in this book revealed the social problematics of American life (class disparities, racial tension, blind patriotism, the outsized power of institutions) in a series of seemingly chance encounters: pallbearers, bikers, politicians, servicemen, miners, families, teenagers, a waitress, and a black maid with a white baby all found their way in front of his lens. Mainstream symbols of American life abound: flags, jukeboxes, cars, televisions, campaign posters, crosses, and the open road (see pages 47–49). Frank's moody photographs, both independently and as members of the extended sequence he made of them in his book, function simultaneously as critique and elegy, suggesting a state of mind caught between fading hope and bitter despair.

Frank made pictures every bit as powerful as Lewis Hine's catalog of faces; as virtuosic as Cartier-Bresson's compositions of arrested time; as unvarnished and descriptive as Walker Evans' balanced observations of place (Evans' 1938 book *American Photographs* was a particularly important influence). But they were somehow different, and Frank's brilliance served a more ambiguous purpose. Reworking the photographic essay, a tool of the socially-concerned photographer, Frank made something less literal and more allusive; something grander and, at the same time, more intimate. With its Homeric conceit—the outsider on a journey through a strange land—and its defeated air, *The Americans* is an epic of American life, told in a minor key.

Frank's book is so richly insightful about society, and so complex in its meanings, that it seems to reject certainty as a first principle. *The Americans* owes its embrace of contingency to its author's understanding of the street as place and subject. Art historian Russell Ferguson characterizes Frank's artistic stance as arising from a kind of purposeful "drifting," as opposed to the "campaigning" of earlier documentary work. [7] Shifting away from traditional framing, resolved symbols, characteristic depictions, and readable narratives of struggle and triumph, Frank made a conscious break from the social realism of his progenitors. He found mystery rather than truth, existential loneliness where predecessors sought a brotherhood of man.

Concurrence: Robert Frank and Garry Winogrand

In late 1955, Robert Frank arrived in Los Angeles, midway through his Guggenheim journey. One day, wandering the neighborhood of Angeleno Heights, he came upon a memorial bronze of Friar Junípero Serra, inexplicably situated on a traffic island on West Sunset Boulevard near Bellevue Avenue. Lifting his Leica to his eye, Frank silhouetted the statue against the sun, so that the pioneering Spanish missionary appeared to raise his cross in futile blessing of the bleak cityscape beyond.

Another young photographer, Garry Winogrand, also traveled cross-country that year from his home in New York. Though he did not yet know Frank or his work, Winogrand too had been profoundly influenced by Walker Evans. As fate would have it, he arrived in

Los Angeles around the same time as Frank, and for a brief period they were both moving about the city, making photographs. One day Winogrand arrived at the statue of Friar Serra: perhaps before Frank, perhaps soon after. He made a mediocre picture of the scene, focusing on the idiosyncrasy of its undistinguished location. Frank, well on his way to making his masterpiece, had produced an extraordinary image; Winogrand was just at the beginning of his career.

Two photographers

In the 1960s, two photographers in particular took street photography in new directions. In purely historical terms, Lee Friedlander and Garry Winogrand were inheritors of Hine and Strand, Cartier-Bresson and Evans, and the photographers of the FSA and the Photo League. However, in the aftermath of Frank, both saw classic social documentary work as a dead end. Neither Friedlander nor Winogrand were idealistic or politically minded in their work; both pursued formal strategies that amounted to a rejection of Modernist aesthetics. Unlike many of their predecessors, Friedlander and Winogrand embraced density of detail, obscurity of meaning, and blankness of content. For them, the chaos of the street was an end in and of itself.

Lee Friedlander, a commercial photographer highly regarded for his album cover portraits of jazz and blues musicians, hit his artistic stride after receiving two Guggenheim Foundation fellowships in the early 1960s. Like Evans before him, Friedlander was a particularist, a visual anthropologist. Unlike Evans, however, he was seemingly interested in the social world only for its formal properties. Friedlander often frames a surfeit

7   Russell Ferguson, "Open City: Possibilities of the Street," in Russell Ferguson and Kerry Brougher, *Open City: Street Photographs Since 1950* (Oxford, England: Museum of Modern Art Oxford, in association with Hatje Cantz Publishers, 2001) 10.

of detail, with a visual complexity that seems to test the boundaries of meaning (see page 57). His pictures are as conceptual as they are documentary in intention: tests of photography's boundless capacity for inclusion —its ability to collect more and more data until, paradoxically, there is nothing there. Mazes of anti-signification, picture puzzles that dismantle social and formal hierarchies, Friedlander's great work is great in direct proportion to the quality of its banality.

Garry Winogrand, a close friend of Friedlander's, reached his artistic maturity in the mid-1960s by producing a torrent of haphazard, disordered images, most made in the middle of crowded city streets (see pages 63–65). Though he learned his trade as a working photojournalist, Winogrand came to reject professional, technical, and formal conventions aimed at producing a straightforward representation of events, instead making pictures that seemed virtually unintentional. Many of his colleagues in journalism derided them as mistakes. Testing the limits of the medium, Winogrand collapsed foregrounds into backgrounds, tilted his camera until the subject seemed to slide out of frame, and aggregated detail until his nominal subject seemed buried amidst multiple points of interest. Winogrand's radical approach seemed to reject the very idea of an ordered universe.

While Winogrand's work is deeply nihilistic in its flouting of meaning and order, it is also richly and darkly humorous. An absurdist at heart, Winogrand was a tragicomic artist in the lineage of Weegee and Klein. He used his camera not to depict the real world but to cast passersby in instant fictional narratives, unintentional *commedia dell-arte* tableaux. He was attracted to spectacle: scenes of confrontation and

Garry Winogrand, *Presidential Candidates' Rally, Statehouse, Providence, R.I.*, 1971

public embarrassment; infirmity, handicaps, and accidents; exaggerated facial expressions and awkward body movements. His best work teases out strange inversions of meaning, recasting reality into a series of symbols that provoke discomforting, or even disturbing thoughts.

The ends of street photography

Some art historians have wondered whether Friedlander and Winogrand have probed the limits of what is possible in street photography. What is left when form overtakes and obscures content, leaving a visual fiction where we expect to find reality? In this viewpoint, the two photographers so authoritatively rejected the genre's origins in social humanism that they laid down a gauntlet for future photographers.

Winogrand's work in particular suggests a philosophical conundrum for the genre. Describing his vision, Winogrand once said that his process succeeds when "the photograph is the most transparent … where there's the least evidence of the hand … where the photographer seemingly exists the least." [8]

On one level, this statement is the canard of a magician using indirection. After all, apparent "artlessness" is as much an aesthetic strategy as any other. On a deeper level, however, Winogrand's statement proposes a disturbing nullity. In his ideal formulation, the photographer vanishes from behind the camera's eye. Not a tool for change, description, or revelation, the camera functions merely as a neutral collector of information, a series of chance encounters between light-sensitive silver and reality. What the lens records has no meaning but that which the viewer ascribes.

Garry Winogrand died of cancer in 1984. In his final years, he bought a motor drive for his Leica camera and had assistants and friends drive him through the streets of Los Angeles, his final home, while he photographed out the car window. The shutter depressed, he captured one instant after another, rarely looking through the rangefinder. In this last stage of his career he literally photographed in disregard of results, not even bothering to process his film, never seeing the images he made. He was like someone playing a slot machine deaf and blind.

Of course, it is impossible to know what Winogrand was thinking during his final years as a photographer. It could be that he was simply trying to develop a new vision, one that could capture a different kind of wide-open street life from that which he had known so well in his longtime home of New York City. It is possible that, had he lived, he would have developed some of his film and edited his final work.

However, it is easy to imagine the opposite: that in fact Winogrand finally took up the gauntlet he had laid down with his nihilistic statement of purpose. That he abrogated, as much as was possible, the role of the author and disappeared from behind the lens. No longer looking for anything, no longer in active rebellion against the moribund aims of socially purposive documentary photography, Winogrand could go no further; and in this, he suggested that he had taken things as far as they could go.

8 Jonathan Green, *American Photography: A Critical History, 1945 to the Present* (New York: Harry Abrams, 1984), 100.

What happens next?

But maybe one can go further.

After all, the streets are still a place where life, in passage, prevails over social structures; where events seemingly take their own shape; where the motion of people becomes a symbolic assertion of freedom. The humanist's concern—a belief in people over systems—remains the core principle of the genre, whether expressed in the committed leftism of Lewis Hine at the genre's beginnings, in the moody existentialism of Robert Frank, or in the aesthetic nihilism of Winogrand and Friedlander. The photographer always brings a certain kind of faith. And yet it is undeniable that street photography has evolved to favor mysteries rather than certainties, seeking the errant, the irresolvable, and the unknown.

Our classic notion of a street photographer is one of a person lying in wait—a hunter of images, full of purpose but dependent on the arrival of prey. Patience awaiting the encounter, followed by a leap to action. The shutter trips open upon recognition of a contingency: a sudden interconnection of forms, an apparent web of relations, an inextricable linkage between movement and meaning. The event is fleeting —change is the only constant in this universe—and life moves on. However, the facts in the frame remain: a trace of the instant is left behind. Chance has favored the prepared mind. The street photographer lowers the camera, keeps moving, and waits for what happens next.

Lewis Hine, *Italian Immigrant, East Side, New York City*, 1910

Paul Strand, *Man, Five Points Square*, 1916

August Sander, *Dachdeckermeister* (Master Roofer), 1930

August Sander, *Fellhändler* (Dealer in Skins), 1930

Henri Cartier-Bresson, *Brussels*, 1932

Walker Evans, *59th Street, New York City* [Onlookers at Bloomingdale's Construction Site], c. 1929–1930

Walker Evans, *Country Store & Gas Station, Alabama* [variant], 1936

Walker Evans, *American Legionnaire*, 1936

Dorothea Lange, *Street Demonstration, San Francisco*, 1934

Weegee (Arthur Fellig), *Wife of Major Green being escorted out of police station,* January 15, 1937

Weegee (Arthur Fellig), "Simply Add Boiling Water," 1937

Weegee (Arthur Fellig), *Norma Devine is Sammy's Mae West* [variant], December 4, 1944

Weegee (Arthur Fellig), "After the Opera … at Sammy's Night Club on the Bowery," c. 1944

Weegee (Arthur Fellig), "Their First Murder," October 9, 1941

Robert Capa, *Chartres, France,* August 18, 1944

Robert Capa, *Naples,* October 2, 1943

Lisette Model, *They Honor Their Sons, New York*, c. 1939–June 14, 1942

Lisette Model, *War Rally, New York*, c. 1941–1942

Lisette Model, *Lower East Side, New York*, c. 1942

Esther Bubley, *On V.E. day a public prayer meeting was held on Main Street. Men are listening to a speech by the school superintendent*, 1945

Robert Frank, *Parade—Hoboken, New Jersey*, 1955

Robert Frank, *U.S. 91, leaving Blackfoot, Idaho*, 1956

Robert Frank, *Trolley—New Orleans*, 1955

Robert Frank, *Coney Island, 4th of July*, 1958

William Klein, *Horn & Hardart, Lexington Avenue*, 1955

Leon Levinstein, *Rockefeller Center*, 1956

Leon Levinstein, *Easter Sunday, 5th Avenue*, 1959

Don Donaghy, *Untitled, New York City*, c. 1960s

Lee Friedlander, *New York City*, 1966

Lee Friedlander, *New York City*, 1963

Ralph Eugene Meatyard, *Romance of Ambrose Bierce #3* [variant], 1964

Lee Friedlander, *Galax, Virginia*, 1962

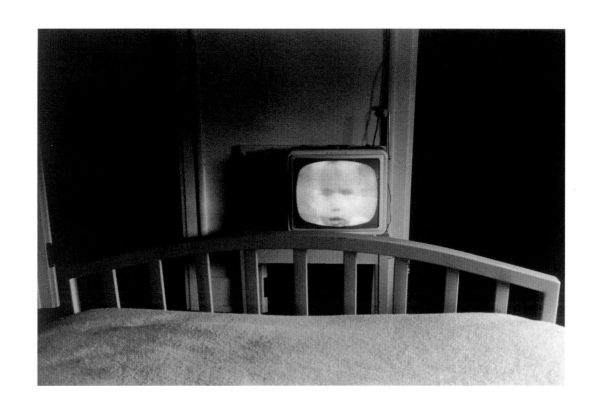

Harry Callahan, *Chicago*, 1961

Diane Arbus, *Burlesque Comedienne, Atlantic City, N.J.*, 1963

Garry Winogrand, *Los Angeles*, 1969

Garry Winogrand, *New York*, c. 1968–1969

Garry Winogrand, *American Legion Convention, Dallas*, 1964

Your eye is a collector.

—Walker Evans

A NOTE ABOUT
THE COLLECTORS
PAUL ROTH

The Walker Evans quotation at left is from a visiting artist lecture with students of the University of Michigan, October 29, 1971. In *Photography: Essays and Images*, ed. Beaumont Newhall (New York: The Museum of Modern Art, 1980), 314.

Norman Carr and Carolyn Kinder Carr began collecting photographs in the late 1970s, an opportune moment for young people of limited means. Great photographs could be acquired at low cost in the early days of the art photography marketplace. Over time, their collection grew to include 159 photographs by such important artists as Diane Arbus, Margaret Bourke-White, Harry Callahan, Robert Capa, Henri Cartier-Bresson, Walker Evans, Robert Frank, Lee Friedlander, Lewis Hine, Dorothea Lange, Leon Levinstein, Lisette Model, Paul Strand, Dan Weiner, and Garry Winogrand. The Carrs acquired the work of legendary tabloid photographer Weegee (Arthur Fellig) in great depth, making him a central figure in their collection. Their 73 photographs constitute one of the best and most comprehensive holdings of his work in private hands.

The Carr Collection is principally built around the history of street photography. Together its pictures provide a rich overview of this important genre, from its origins in the early years of the 20th century through the 1980s. The collection includes many important works and undisputed masterpieces, but it also holds surprises. Photographers who are not generally considered street photographers, such as August Sander and Ralph Eugene Meatyard, appear in a new light when considered alongside acknowledged contributors to the form. Some of the Carrs' best photographs are chosen from the cutting edge of an artist's work rather than their center.

While building their collection, the Carrs reared two children and pursued careers well-matched to their avocations. After graduating from Amherst College, Norman Carr studied law at Columbia University, and then began a 40-year career as a trial lawyer in Akron, Ohio. His tenacity, patience, and critical intelligence—useful in his legal career—are of equal value in art collecting. Over time, he developed a penetrating eye, engaged in serious research, and acquired the persistence needed to build a survey collection.

Carolyn Kinder Carr, an art historian, is Deputy Director and Chief Curator of the National Portrait Gallery in Washington, D.C. A graduate of Smith College, she received her MA from Oberlin College and her PhD from Case Western Reserve University. Carolyn has organized numerous exhibitions for the Portrait Gallery. Recent projects include *Hans Namuth: Portraits*, *Alice Neel: Women*, *Retratos: 2000 Years of Latin American Portraits*, and *Legacy: Spain and the United States in the Age of Independence, 1763–1848*. Prior to joining the Portrait Gallery, she taught art history at Kent State University and the University of Akron, and was chief curator at the Akron Art Museum in Ohio from 1978 to 1983.

The best photography collectors build their holdings with the same passion, concentration, and motivation that art historians bring to the writing of books or the organization of exhibitions. The Carr Collection is more than a group of pictures: it is an assemblage of distinct documentary and artistic visions that chronicle the evolution of a genre.

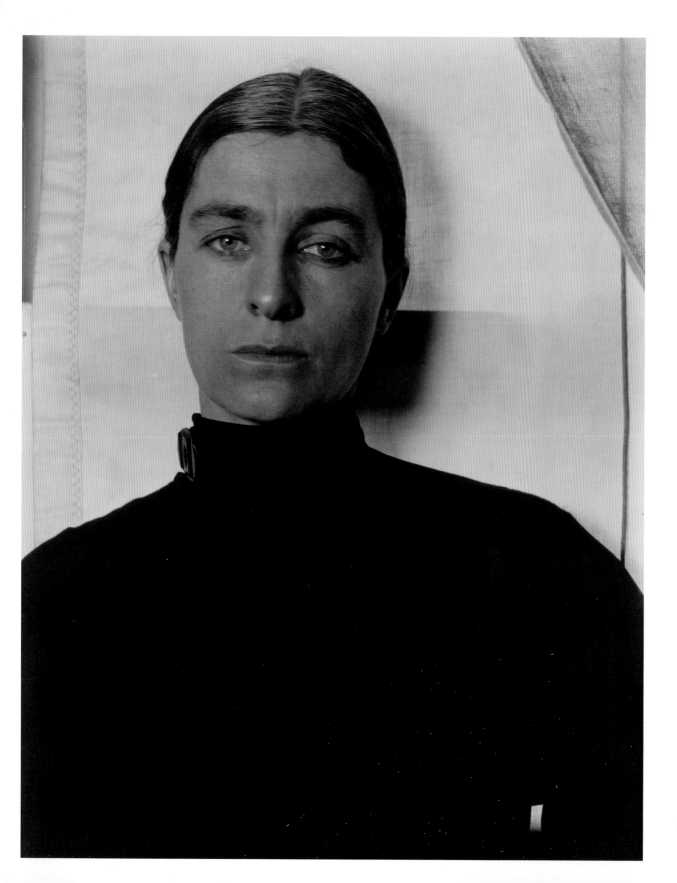

Paul Strand, *Rebecca Strand*, c. 1928–1929

We do not profess to be experts about the nature of photography collecting. We could suggest that one commonality among collectors is the desire to be surrounded by extraordinary objects. Another might be the desire for proximity to the creative act. The aspiration to be a concert pianist or an opera singer is unrealistic unless one has substantial musical gifts; to be a photographer seems well within the realm of possibility. Most photography collectors have owned and used cameras. Nevertheless, the ability to make a compelling image is rare, demanding another level of insight and expertise.

We have always been interested in art and, shortly after we were married, we began collecting, albeit on a limited budget. Our initial acquisitions were limited edition prints and the works of close friends who were artists. It was John Coplans, curator and founding editor of *Artforum*, who introduced us to the history of photography and encouraged us to become serious photography collectors. At the time, Norman was a trial lawyer in Akron, Ohio, and was active with several cultural boards, including that of the Akron Art Museum. Carolyn, who had taught art history courses at the university level and served as the art critic for the local newspaper, was in the final stages of obtaining her PhD.

We met John in 1978 when he was looking for a job. He and *Artforum* had been sued for libel over an article that John had written narrating the many difficulties he had encountered as director of the Pasadena Art Museum. Norman led the Akron Art Museum's search committee for a new director, which convinced John to come to Akron (to the heart of the "American Ruhr," as he called it). He stayed less than two years before leaving to reinvent himself as a photographer.

We became very close to John. He subsequently hired Carolyn (who had finished her PhD at Case Western Reserve University) as Chief Curator of the Akron Art Museum. With his impeccable sense of what was important in contemporary art and photography, John brought national stature to this small institution in a short period of time. If genius is defined as the capacity to have unusual insights that are incisive and apt, then John was a genius— one of the few we have known.

Carolyn began organizing photographic shows for the museum, and Norman, on John's advice, began looking at a wide range of books on photography. At that point, John's own collection consisted of mammoth-plate albumen prints of Yosemite by Carleton Watkins and some rare prints by Arthur Fellig, better known as Weegee. In 1977, John had organized the first major museum exhibition of Weegee's work for the International Center of Photography. Subsequently, we acquired his photographs by Weegee; the J. Paul Getty Museum now owns the photographs by Watkins.

Though John got us started collecting photographs, we did not consult him on individual purchases. He did, however, introduce us to important figures in the field, among them Weston Naef (then with the Metropolitan Museum of Art, now with the J. Paul Getty Museum), and John Waddell, whose collection was eventually purchased by the Metropolitan in 1989. Initially, we sought to compare the quality of the pictures we were interested in buying with those we saw in rotating installations drawn from the permanent collection at the Museum of Modern Art in New York. We aspired to find images that were on that level. At the few photography galleries then in operation, we would educate ourselves by spending hours going through dozens of really fine images and conversing at length with the dealers, who were delighted to speak to anyone with a genuine interest in the medium.

From the beginning, we were in New York frequently. We bought at auctions and we met various dealers, among them Peter MacGill, who had not yet established his own gallery, but was working for the Light Gallery. In Washington, D.C., where we moved in 1984, we got to know dealers Gerd Sander and Harry Lunn, who opened his first small gallery in Georgetown in 1971 and pioneered new methods of marketing photography, notably with the work of Ansel Adams. It was all new in those days for both dealers and collectors, and the field was wide open for neophytes like us. One dealer we worked with in New York City, Howard Greenberg, started his first gallery with no commercial backing over a coffee shop in Woodstock in 1977. Jeffrey Fraenkel, a dealer in San Francisco from whom we purchased several photographs over the years, came to represent Garry Winogrand by writing him an unsolicited (but successful) letter in 1979, stating that he was opening a new gallery and wanted him to join his roster.

The photography market was much smaller and more personal than it is now. The first important purchases we made from Peter MacGill arrived with handwritten notes describing the beauty and significance of each image. The earliest accompanied Paul Strand's portrait of his then-wife, Rebecca (see page 68). Peter's letter read, in part: "The picture was made in a fraction of a second yet it depicts a penetrating aspect of Rebecca's personality. Stieglitz was fascinated by this concept and found it manifest in Strand's work." For us, the Strand *Rebecca* is remarkably beautiful and not something that one would leave behind or forget having seen.

Our collection runs chronologically from British photographer Roger Fenton (1819–1869) to Washington-based photographer and collagist Joseph Mills (born 1951), although most of our photographs are from the 20th century. We never thought the collection should be rigidly limited to one kind of work, but we did begin to focus increasingly on those artists whose work either falls into the category of street photography, such as Robert Frank, or directly relates to the human condition, as is the case with Diane Arbus. Those were the photographs that moved us most as we were learning the history of the medium.

Our subject concentration also helped us refine the quality of our collection. It is often difficult to discern the true vintage of a photographic print, because different rules apply to every photographer; but by limiting ourselves to a few key works by a few important artists, it was possible for us to do intense research before making purchases. We also sought to establish the provenance of our acquisitions whenever possible—not an easy task as photographers often made multiple prints of an image. But once in Washington, we found the city's museums and libraries to be excellent resources. In many instances, they have made it possible for us to glean information unknown to the seller or auction house experts. On other occasions, curators and historians have been generous in sharing their extensive knowledge with us.

From the beginning, dealer expertise has played a significant role in our decision-making. When we were considering a beautiful vintage print of Walker Evans' *Country Store & Gas Station, Alabama* (see page 31), Peter MacGill was able to demonstrate that this particular print had been a gift from Evans to writer James Agee, who collaborated with the photographer on *Let Us Now Praise Famous Men* in 1936. A letter from Agee's widow Mia established its history.

Sometimes persistent probing was required. In the case of *Brussels* by Henri Cartier-Bresson (see page 29), we believed that we were looking at a very early print; but we had no idea what a vintage print by Cartier-Bresson would look like. At the time, we knew of no dealer in the country with that information. The photograph was offered by a small gallery in Canada: they had several early works by Cartier-Bresson, all obtained from renowned art dealer Julien Levy. At our request the gallery contacted Levy, who confirmed in writing on the verso that he had used this very print in his landmark book *Surrealism* (1936). The original size notation on the back, also in his handwriting, matches the size of the image in the book.

Serendipity is part of the process as well. When we acquired Robert Frank's *U.S. 91, leaving Blackfoot, Idaho* (see page 48) at auction in 1981, we paid no attention to the publication stamp on the print verso. Twenty years later, Paul Roth, then associate curator of photography and media arts at the Corcoran Gallery of Art and former archivist of the Robert Frank Collection at the National Gallery of Art, recognized the stamp and identified the print as the one used to reproduce the image in *U.S. Camera 1958,* the magazine annual where Frank first published pictures from his book *The Americans* (1959). This meant that our photograph was produced very early, one of the first Frank made.

We purchased Diane Arbus' *Burlesque Comedienne, Atlantic City, N.J.* (see page 62) at auction in 1983. We immediately recognized that it was a vintage print. Not only was it signed and dated in Arbus' hand on the verso, but the lot included the photograph's original enclosure, a glassine envelope inscribed by Arbus with her signature and a salutation to the recipient:

"Dear Sol, The First." After the auction, we were amused when several people contacted us wanting to buy the envelope. Years later, after the 1995 publication of the book *Untitled* (which featured her final major project), we approached the dealer for the Arbus Estate hoping to acquire one or more prints. Comparing the few available vintage examples side-by-side with the ones printed posthumously was a real education about Arbus' unique and expressive printing style. We chose a vintage print of *Untitled (18)*. The Arbus Estate confirmed that it was unique, the only print of this image that Arbus made (see page 79).

After we moved to Washington, our collecting became less active for a number of years. This changed in 1992, when Jane Livingston, then chief curator at the Corcoran Gallery of Art, produced a book devoted to New York street photography, *The New York School: Photographs 1936–1963*. It was apparent to us that some important photographers were missing from our collection. Howard Greenberg owned a great deal of the material, so a comparative review was easy. After determining our options—much like a museum curator planning an exhibition or weighing acquisition alternatives—we isolated Leon Levinstein as a photographer we should add to our collection. We now own three rare examples of his work. Some years later, we acquired another photographer from the New York School, Don Donaghy, when we located one of the vintage prints Livingston had originally exhibited, still on its Corcoran mount.

Of course, we were not always successful in getting what we wanted. Early on, Norman decided Ralph Steiner would be an important addition to the collection, because he had so clearly influenced Walker Evans. We discovered that he lived less than 20 miles from the town in New Hampshire where Norman had grown up. We wrote asking if he had any vintage prints we could look at. He replied that his earliest prints were junk—poorly printed—and that numerous cats slept on them. We never did get a Steiner.

Looking back on the timing of our experience, it is clear that the first few years of our collecting constituted the end of a unique, never-to-be-replicated period for acquiring photographs. We are fortunate to have begun collecting in 1979. At the time, only a limited number of museums, dealers, and private individuals were collecting photographs. When we first bought work at Christie's East, we had no idea that photography auctions were uncommon in New York until the late 1970s. Nor did we know that this early era, in which the best photographs were still fairly inexpensive, was about to end. At the time, the quality of the available material from masters such as Diane Arbus, Walker Evans, Robert Frank, Weegee, and Garry Winogrand vastly exceeded the serious collector pool, whereas the precise opposite seems to be true at the present time.

Collecting art is a controlled obsession. Today the challenge for serious photography collectors is to locate great material—within reach—that emotionally involves them. With the right measure of passion, diligence, and knowledge, building a great collection is still a possibility worth every effort.

Weegee (Arthur Fellig), "Crowd at Coney Island, Temperature 89 degrees … They came early, and stayed late," July 22, 1940

CATALOG OF
THE COLLECTION OF
NORMAN CARR AND
CAROLYN KINDER CARR

Asterisk (*) denotes photographs
included in the exhibition *Chance
Encounters: Photographs from the
Collection of Norman Carr and
Carolyn Kinder Carr*

BERENICE ABBOTT (1898–1991)

1 * *Flatiron Building*, c. 1930-1933
gelatin silver print, 9 3/16 × 7 7/16 in.

DIANE ARBUS (1923–1971)

2 * *Burlesque Comedienne, Atlantic City, N.J.*, 1963
gelatin silver print, 9 1/2 × 9 5/16 in.

3 * *Untitled (7)*, 1970-1971
gelatin silver print, 15 1/8 × 14 11/16 in.

4 * *Untitled (18)*, 1970-1971
gelatin silver print, 15 3/4 × 15 3/16 in.

MARGARET BOURKE-WHITE (1904–1971)

5 * Untitled, c. 1930s
gelatin silver print, 2 7/8 × 3 15/16 in.

ESTHER BUBLEY (1921–1998)

6 * *On V.E. day a public prayer meeting was held on
Main Street. Men are listening to a speech by the
school superintendent*, 1945
gelatin silver print, 10 1/2 × 10 1/4 in.

7 * [*Main Street. Saturday afternoon. Shoppers*], 1945
gelatin silver print, 10 1/2 × 10 1/4 in.

HARRY CALLAHAN (1912–1999)

8 * *Chicago*, 1948
gelatin silver print, 13 3/4 × 9 15/16 in.

9 *Chicago*, c. 1950
gelatin silver print, 8 × 10 in.

10 * *Chicago*, 1961
gelatin silver print, 9 1/2 × 6 5/16 in.

11 *Eleanor and Barbara, Chicago*, 1954
gelatin silver print, 6 5/8 × 6 9/16 in.

12 *Wales*, 1984
dye transfer print, 9 5/8 × 14 3/8 in.

ROBERT CAPA (1913–1954)

13 * *Chartres, France*, August 18, 1944
gelatin silver print, 8 7/16 × 12 1/2 in.

14 * *Madrid*, November–December 1936
gelatin silver print, 6 7/8 × 10 1/2 in.

15 * *Naples*, October 2, 1943
gelatin silver print, 10 × 13 11/16 in.

HENRI CARTIER-BRESSON (1908–2004)

16 * *Brussels*, 1932
gelatin silver print, 6 5/8 × 9 7/8 in.

17 *Shanghai*, 1949
gelatin silver print, 7 3/4 × 11 7/8 in.

JOHN COPLANS (1920–2003)

18 *Back with Arms Above*, 1984
gelatin silver print, 21 1/2 × 17 in.

19 *Norman Carr*, 1978-1979
color coupler (chromogenic) print, 10 7/8 × 10 3/4 in.

20 *Norman Carr*, 1978-1979
gelatin silver print, 10 9/16 × 10 1/2 in.

21 *Norman Carr*, 1978-1979
gelatin silver print, 17 × 13 in.

22 Untitled [Self-Portrait], 1978-1979
gelatin silver print, 9 7/16 × 10 3/8 in.

23 Untitled [Self-Portrait], 1980
gelatin silver print, 15 × 15 in.

DON DONAGHY (1936–)

24 *Philadelphia*, 1962
gelatin silver print, 4 5/8 × 6 15/16 in.

25 * *Untitled, New York City*, c. 1960s
gelatin silver print, 13 1/2 × 9 1/8 in.

ELLIOTT ERWITT (1928–)

26 *Untitled, New York*, 1946
gelatin silver print, 7 3/4 × 11 3/4 in.

KÁROLY ESCHER (1890–1966)

27 * *Napsugaras tavasz a korzón* (Sunlit spring day on the promenade)
[variant], c. 1930
gelatin silver print, 9 1/4 × 7 in.
Corcoran Gallery of Art, Gift of Norman S. and Carolyn K. Carr

WALKER EVANS (1903–1975)

28 * *American Legionnaire*, 1936
gelatin silver print, 6 1/8 × 9 1/4 in.

29 * *Country Store & Gas Station, Alabama* [variant], 1936
gelatin silver print, 5 15/16 × 7 5/16 in.

30 * *59th Street, New York City* [Onlookers at Bloomingdale's
Construction Site], c. 1929-1930
gelatin silver print, 7 3/16 × 10 11/16 in.

ROGER FENTON (1819–1869)

31 *Colin Campbell, 1st Baron Clyde, 1792-1863. Field-Marshal*
[variant], c. 1855
salt print, 8 1/2 × 6 13/16 in.

ABE FRAJNDLICH (1946–)

32 *"Ball Busters," 203 Park Ave.*, 1976
gelatin silver print, 18 3/16 × 12 3/8 in.

33 *Hats, Scarves and a Chain, 203 Park Ave.*, 1976,
gelatin silver print, 10 5/8 × 15 5/8 in.

34 *In Robert Heinecken's Stetson, 203 Park Ave.*, 1976
gelatin silver print, 11 7/8 × 17 1/2 in.

35 *Mirror, 203 Park Ave.*, 1976
gelatin silver print, 12 1/4 × 18 5/16 in.

ROBERT FRANK (1924–)

36 * *Coney Island, 4th of July*, 1958
gelatin silver print, 16 15/16 × 13 1/6 in.

37 *Hoover Dam, Nevada*, 1955
gelatin silver print, 12 × 4 1/2 in.

38 *Italian Women in Venice*, 1949
gelatin silver print, 7 × 9 3/8 in.

39 *New York City* (From the Bus), 1958
gelatin silver print, 9 1/4 × 6 1/4 in.

40 * *Parade—Hoboken, New Jersey*, 1955
gelatin silver print, 15 1/4 × 23 in.

41   *Salt Lake City, Utah*, 1956
gelatin silver print, 10 1/2 × 7 in.

42 * *Trolley—New Orleans*, 1955
gelatin silver print, 9 × 13 1/2 in.

43 * Untitled [Peru], 1948
gelatin silver print, 13 1/2 × 10 in.

44   Untitled [Peru], 1948
gelatin silver print, 12 15/16 × 8 9/16 in.

45 * *U.S. 91, leaving Blackfoot, Idaho*, 1956
gelatin silver print, 8 11/16 × 13 3/16 in.
[alternate title, on print verso: *Butte, Montana,
Copper Miners Going to Work*]

LEE FRIEDLANDER (1934–)

46 * *Galax, Virginia*, 1962
gelatin silver print, 5 7/8 × 8 7/8 in.

47 * *New York City*, 1963
gelatin silver print, 6 1/4 × 9 5/16 in.

48 * *New York City*, 1966
gelatin silver print, 6 5/16 × 9 1/2 in.

49   *Sonora Desert, Arizona*, 1995
gelatin silver print, 14 9/16 × 14 3/4 in.

50   *Paris, France*, 1997
gelatin silver print, 14 15/16 × 14 13/16 in.

51   *Paris, France*, 1997
gelatin silver print, 15 × 14 7/8 in.

LEWIS HINE (1874–1940)

52 * *Italian Immigrant, East Side, New York City*, 1910
gelatin silver print, 5 × 7 in.

53   *Juvenile Court, St. Louis, Missouri*, May 5, 1910
gelatin silver print, 3 1/2 × 4 1/2 in.

WILLIAM KLEIN (1928–)

54 * *Horn & Hardart, Lexington Avenue*, 1955
gelatin silver print, 9 5/16 × 14 7/8 in.

DOROTHEA LANGE (1895–1965)

55 * *Street Demonstration, San Francisco*, 1934
gelatin silver print, 13 5/8 × 10 1/2 in.

LEON LEVINSTEIN (1913–1988)

56 * *Easter Sunday, 5th Avenue*, 1959
gelatin silver print, 11 1/8 × 16 1/4 in.

57 * *Rockefeller Center*, 1956
gelatin silver print, 16 1/2 × 13 13/16 in.

58   Untitled, c. 1954
gelatin silver print, 10 7/8 × 13 7/8 in.

O. WINSTON LINK (1914–2001)

59   *Hawkshill Creek Swimming Hole, Luray, Virginia*, 1956
gelatin silver print, 19 7/16 × 15 5/8 in.

60   *Old Maud Bows to the Virginia Creeper*, 1956
gelatin silver print, 15 9/16 × 19 3/8 in.

RALPH EUGENE MEATYARD (1925–1972)

61 * *Romance of Ambrose Bierce #3* [variant], 1964
gelatin silver print, 6 1/2 × 7 1/4 in.

JOEL MEYEROWITZ (1938–)

62   *Hartwig House, Truro*, 1976
color coupler (chromogenic) print, 15 × 9 1/2 in.

JOE MILLS (1951–)

63   Untitled, c. 1980s
varnished gelatin silver print mounted on wood
17 11/16 × 11 13/16 in.

64 * *Untitled, Washington, D.C.*, c. 1982–1989
varnished gelatin silver print mounted on suitcase lid
17 11/16 × 11 13/16 in.

LISETTE MODEL (1901–1983)

65 * *Lower East Side, New York*, c. 1942
gelatin silver print, 13 5/8 × 10 7/8 in.

66 * *They Honor Their Sons, New York*, c. 1939–June 14, 1942
gelatin silver print, 14 × 11 in.

67 * *War Rally, New York*, c. 1941–1942
gelatin silver print, 13 9/16 × 10 9/16 in.

IRVING PENN (1917–)

68   *Georgia O'Keeffe*, 1948
palladium print, 22 15/16 × 17 3/8 in.

THURMAN ROTAN (1903–1991)

69   Untitled, c. 1930s
gelatin silver print, 4 1/2 × 3 1/2 in.

AUGUST SANDER (1876–1964)

70 * *Dachdeckermeister* (Master Roofer), 1930
gelatin silver print, 11 3/8 × 9 in.

71 * *Fellhändler* (Dealer in Skins), 1930
gelatin silver print, 11 × 7 7/8 in.

72 * *Grobschmied* (Blacksmith), 1913
gelatin silver print, 11 × 8 3/4 in.

PAUL STRAND (1890–1976)

73 * *Man, Five Points Square*, 1916
photogravure, 6 11/16 × 7 7/16 in.

74 * *Rebecca Strand*, c. 1928–1929
gelatin silver print, 10 × 8 in.

WEEGEE (ARTHUR FELLIG) (1899–1968)

For Weegee, original publication captions are enclosed in quotation
marks; photograph titles are italicized.

75 * "A couple driven out from the burning tenement…," April 23, 1944
gelatin silver print, 13 1/2 × 10 7/16 in.

76 * "After the Opera … at Sammy's Night Club on the Bowery," c. 1944
gelatin silver print, 13 9/16 × 10 9/16 in.

77   "And a girl smiles too … Then she cries … The Swoon," [variant],
November 5, 1944
gelatin silver print, 10 1/2 × 13 3/8 in.

78 * *Anthony Esposito, Accused "Cop Killer*," January 16, 1941
gelatin silver print, 13 5/8 × 10 11/16 in.

79   *Anthony Esposito, Accused "Cop Killer"* [variant], January 16, 1941
two gelatin silver prints, 6 1/2 × 4 5/8 in. each

80   *At the Palace Theatre*, c. 1943
gelatin silver print, 13 9/16 × 10 11/16 in.

81   *At the Palace Theatre II*, c. 1943
gelatin silver print, 13 × 10 5/8 in.

Diane Arbus, *Untitled (18)*, 1970–1971